Crème Brûlée

First published in Great Britain in 2003 by Hamlyn
This edition published in 2014 by Spruce
a division of Octopus Publishing Group Ltd
Endeavour House, 189 Shaftesbury Avenue, London, WC2H 8JY
www.octopusbooks.co.uk
www.octopusbooksusa.com

An Hachette UK Company www.hachette.co.uk

Distributed in the US by Hachette Book Group USA
237 Park Avenue, New York NY 10017 USA

Distributed in Canada by Canadian Manda Group
165 Dufferin Street, Toronto, Ontario, Canada M6K 3H6

ISBN 978 1 84601 479 6
A CIP catalogue record for this book is available from the British Library
Printed and bound in China

10 9 8 7 6 5 4 3 2 1

Consultant Publisher Sarah Ford
Design Eoghan O'Brien and Michelle Tilly
Photographer Jeremy Hopley
Food Styling Annie Nichols
Production Controller Sarah-Jayne Johnson

Notes

Medium eggs have been used throughout.

A few recipes include nuts or nut derivatives. It is advisable for those with known allergic reactions to nuts and nut derivatives and those who may be potentially vulnerable to these allergies, such as pregnant and nursing mothers, invalids, the elderly, babies, and children, to avoid dishes made with nuts and nut oils. It is also prudent to check the labels of prepared ingredients for the possible inclusion of nut derivatives.

Pepper should be freshly ground black pepper unless otherwise stated.

Ovens should be preheated to the specified temperature. If using a convection oven, follow the manufacturer's instructions for adjusting the time and temperature.

Crème Brûlée

THE WORLD'S "*most famous*" DESSERT

spruce

Contents

Introduction

Crème brûlées have been popular since the mid-17th century when they were favored by the French, English, and Spanish aristocracies. There is much debate about their origin, but possibly they developed simultaneously in several European countries.

Now found at good restaurants all over the world, brûlées are as popular as ever. Yet these rich little elegant dishes are surprisingly easy to make, especially if you have a hand-held blowtorch to caramelize the sugar topping. Finished in a matter of minutes, the crisp brittle topping elevates a simple baked custard to a gourmet feast. Crack the sugar with the edge of a teaspoon for maximum dramatic effect then scoop down to the sensuously rich, creamy, baked custard underneath.

For those who have never made a brûlée before, this book takes you carefully through each step, while for those more experienced cooks there are some exotic flavor combinations to enjoy, both sweet

and savoury, including Lobster and Tarragon or Raspberry and Champagne.

THE INGREDIENTS
Since the ingredients needed for a brûlée are few and simple, it makes sense to choose the best quality; after all, the finished dish can only be as good as the items that have gone into it.

Cream Traditionally made with heavy cream to create a rich, creamy custard, brûlées can also be made with a combination of milk and other creams such as clotted cream or crème fraîche, or even with the soft Italian cream cheese mascarpone. For a lighter custard, light cream, sour cream, or buttermilk are delicious alternatives.

Eggs All the recipes in this book have been made with medium-sized eggs. Always check the date stamp before using them and separate the eggs carefully.

Sugar Traditionally, superfine or finely granulated sugar are the easiest to use when making custard and are ideal sprinkled over the top of baked custards prior to caramelizing. Confectioner's sugar, light brown sugar, and demerara or raw sugar may also be used for the caramelized topping.

EQUIPMENT

Baking dishes All the recipes in this book have been made in ¾ cup or 3¾ x 1¾ inch individual ovenproof china ramekins or custard cups. Individual glass or ceramic soufflé dishes may also be used.

Bain marie To prevent the custard from baking too quickly, the brûlées are cooked in a bain marie or water bath. Place the ramekins or custard cups in a roasting pan or shallow casserole, then pour in warm water to come halfway up the sides of the individual dishes.

Fine sieve This is essential for straining flavorings from cooled cream and to remove any threads of egg after making custard. Choose one with a stainless steel or fine nylon mesh.

Blowtorches There are two types available; one is powered with lighter fuel, the second with a butane gas canister. Both are very efficient and easy to use, heating up quickly to a staggeringly hot 2700°F.

Salamander These have a long handle with a metal disc attached. This is heated in a gas flame and pressed onto the sugar in much the same way as a branding iron is used.

YOUR QUESTIONS ANSWERED

The custard has overheated . . . help!
Don't panic if the custard overheats. Quickly stop the cooking either by plunging the base of the pan into a bowl of cold water, adding a frozen picnic ice pack to help lower the temperature still more and whisking the custard vigorously with a hand-held balloon whisk. Alternatively, pour the custard into a food processor and blend until smooth; strain it through a fine sieve then take stock of the damage. Hopefully the custard will look silky smooth once more; if not you may have to admit defeat and throw it away.

Can I make crème brûlée the day before my friends come to dinner?
Yes; if anything custard bases seem to improve the longer they are chilled. The suggested times of 3–4 hours are a minimum recommendation and, if it helps you to spread your work load, then make and bake the desserts the night before, but don't add the sugar topping until just before serving, or it will dissolve.

Can I make the caramel topping separately?
Line a baking tray with foil and, using an empty upturned custard cup, draw around the top of the dish. Brush the foil lightly with a little sunflower oil or butter then sprinkle 1–2 teaspoons of sugar in an even layer inside each circle. Caramelize the circles with a blowtorch. Leave the sugared discs to cool then simply peel them off the foil and put them on top of the chilled custards just before serving. Alternatively follow the method on page 44.

What about leftover egg whites?
Pack egg whites in small plastic containers in amounts that you are most likely to use for angel food cake or meringues. Seal well, label, and freeze for up to 3 months. Defrost in the refrigerator overnight and use in the normal way. Alternatively you can store them in a covered bowl in the refrigerator for up to 3 days.

Glossary

US	**UK**
all-purpose flour	plain flour
confectioner's sugar	icing sugar
cornstarch	cornflour
golden raisins	sultanas
heavy cream	double cream
light cream	single cream
pie weights	baking beans
scallions	spring onions
skillet	frying pan
superfine sugar	caster sugar

Conversion Table

Standard American cup measurements are used in all recipes.

¼ cup = 60 ml (2 fl oz)
⅓ cup = 75 ml (3 fl oz)
½ cup = 120 ml (4 fl oz)
1 cup = 240 ml (8 fl oz)

1 stick of butter = 120 g (4 oz)

Vanilla Bean CRÈME BRÛLÉE

THIS CLASSIC FRENCH DESSERT IS POPULAR ALL OVER THE WORLD. SERVE IT SIMPLY BY ITSELF OR WITH RASPBERRIES, STRAWBERRIES, AND MINT LEAVES DUSTED WITH CONFECTIONER'S SUGAR.

1 vanilla bean
2½ cups heavy cream
8 egg yolks
¼ cup superfine sugar
3 tablespoons confectioner's sugar

Tip
One teaspoon of vanilla extract can be added to the egg yolks in place of a vanilla bean in the cream.

1. Slit the vanilla bean lengthwise and put it in a saucepan. Pour the cream into the pan, then bring almost to a boil. Take off the heat and allow to stand for 15 minutes for the vanilla flavor to develop.

2. Lift the vanilla bean out of the cream and, holding it against the side of the saucepan, scrape the black seeds into the cream. Discard the bean casing.

3. Use a fork to mix together the egg yolks and superfine sugar in a bowl. Reheat the cream, then gradually mix it into the egg yolks and sugar. Strain the mixture back into the saucepan.

4. Place 6 ovenproof ramekins or custard cups in a roasting pan, then divide the custard between them. Pour warm water around the dishes to come halfway up the sides, then bake in a preheated oven at 350°F for 20–25 minutes until the custards are just set with a slight softness at the center.

5. Leave the dishes to cool in the water, then lift them out and chill in the refrigerator for 3–4 hours. About 25 minutes before serving, sprinkle the tops with confectioner's sugar (no need to sift). Caramelize using a blowtorch, then leave at room temperature.

CREMA
CATALANA

MADE WITH MILK, THIS SPANISH FAVORITE IS LIGHTER THAN A CLASSIC CRÈME BRÛLÉE. THE TOPPING IS TRADITIONALLY MADE WITH A SALAMANDER, A METAL DISK WITH A LONG HANDLE THAT IS HEATED ON AN OPEN FLAME, THEN PRESSED ONTO THE SUGAR.

5 egg yolks
⅓ cup superfine sugar
2 tablespoons cornstarch
2½ cups whole milk
¼ teaspoon ground cinnamon
large pinch freshly grated nutmeg
1 small lemon, finely grated zest only
⅓ cup demerara or raw sugar

Tip
Grated orange zest may also be used instead of the lemon zest, or a cinnamon stick instead of the ground cinnamon, but make sure you remove the cinnamon stick before pouring the custard into the serving dishes.

1. Put the egg yolks, superfine sugar, and cornstarch in a bowl and use a fork to mix together until smooth.

2. Pour the milk into a saucepan, add the cinnamon, nutmeg, and lemon zest and bring to a boil. Gradually stir the spiced milk into the egg yolk mixture, then pour the milk mixture back into the saucepan and bring to a boil, stirring continuously. Reduce the heat and cook for 2–3 minutes, still stirring, until the custard has thickened.

3. Pour the custard into 4 shallow 1¼-cup ceramic dishes and leave to cool. Transfer to the refrigerator for 3–4 hours. About 20–30 minutes before serving, sprinkle the desserts with the demerara sugar, caramelize with a blowtorch, then leave at room temperature until ready to serve.

Sweet
RICE PUDDING
BRÛLÉE

SOFT GRAINS OF COOKED RICE ARE BATHED IN A WONDERFULLY RICH VANILLA CUSTARD HIDDEN BENEATH A BITTERSWEET BRITTLE CARAMEL—THIS IS COMFORT FOOD AT ITS VERY BEST.

2 cups whole milk
½ cup risotto rice
¼ cup superfine sugar
4 egg yolks
1 cup heavy cream
1 teaspoon vanilla extract
¼ cup superfine sugar, to finish

Tip
These puddings can be eaten cold, but as they cool the rice swells to make a much firmer finish.

1. Pour the milk into a saucepan, bring to a boil, then add the rice. Reduce the heat and cook over a moderate heat for 15 minutes, stirring occasionally until the rice is soft and about one-third of the milk remains.

2. Take the saucepan off the heat and stir in the sugar. Use a fork to mix together the egg yolks, cream, and vanilla extract in a bowl, then strain into the rice and mix well.

3. Arrange 6 heatproof ramekins or custard cups in a roasting pan. Spoon the rice and custard into the dishes, then pour warm water into the roasting pan to come halfway up the sides of the dishes. Bake in a preheated oven at 350°F for 20–25 minutes until the custard is just set.

4. Leave the dishes to cool in the water for 40–50 minutes. Lift out, sprinkle the tops with sugar, and caramelize with a blowtorch. Serve within 20–30 minutes.

Bread
AND BUTTER
BRÛLÉE

THIS RECIPE IS A WONDERFUL VERSION OF TRADITIONAL BREAD AND BUTTER PUDDING—COMFORTINGLY SWEET AND BURNISHED TO A DEEP GOLDEN BROWN WITH A SOFT VANILLA CUSTARD SPECKLED WITH MOIST GOLDEN RAISINS BENEATH.

10 slices white bread
¼ cup (½ stick) butter, at room temperature
a little freshly grated nutmeg
½ cup golden raisins
8 egg yolks
½ cup superfine sugar
½ teaspoon vanilla extract
1 cup heavy cream
1½ cups whole milk
6 tablespoons superfine sugar, to finish

1. Spread the bread thinly with butter, then trim off the crusts and cut each slice into four triangles. Butter 6 shallow oval or rectangular individual ovenproof dishes, each about 1¼ cups. Arrange a flat layer of bread triangles in the base of each one. Sprinkle lightly with nutmeg and divide the golden raisins between the dishes. Arrange the remaining bread triangles, overlapping in a line over the top of the first layer. Place the dishes in two roasting pans.

2. Use a fork to mix together the egg yolks, sugar, and vanilla extract in a bowl. Pour the cream and milk into a saucepan and bring to a boil. Gradually beat into the egg yolk mixture, then strain into the bread-filled dishes. Allow to stand for 10 minutes for the bread to soak up the custard.

3. Pour warm water into the roasting pans, to come halfway up the sides of the dishes. Cover the pans loosely with buttered foil and bake the puddings in a preheated oven at 350°F for 20–25 minutes until the custards are set around the edges.

4. Take the dishes out of the roasting pans and remove the foil. Sprinkle the tops of the puddings liberally with the remaining sugar, then caramelize with a blowtorch. Serve warm.

APPLE
PIE BRÛLÉE

ALL THE CREAMY SMOOTHNESS OF A CLASSIC BRÛLÉE CUSTARD BAKED IN A CRISP BUTTERY PIE SHELL AND TOPPED WITH CARAMELIZED APPLE SLICES.

Pie shell
1½ cups all-purpose flour
½ cup (1 stick) butter, diced
3 tablespoons water

Filling
2 dessert apples, peeled, cored, and chopped
2 tablespoons water
6 egg yolks
¼ cup superfine sugar
1½ cups heavy cream

Topping
1 dessert apple, cored, thinly sliced, and tossed in
1 tablespoon lemon juice
¼ cup superfine sugar

1. Put the flour in a bowl with the butter, and rub in with the fingers until it resembles breadcrumbs. Mix in enough water to make a smooth dough. Knead lightly, then cut into 5 pieces. Roll 1 piece out thinly and use to line 4-inch, removable bottom mini tart pans. Trim off the excess and reserve. When you have lined 5 pans, use the trimmings for the sixth. Chill for 15 minutes.

2. Put the pans on a baking tray, line the tarts with squares of wax paper and fill with pie weights. Bake in a preheated oven at 375°F for 10 minutes. Remove the paper and weights and cook for a further 5 minutes. Reduce the oven temperature to 350°F.

3. Put the apples in a saucepan with the water, cover, and cook gently for 10 minutes until soft. Mash until smooth. Use a fork to mix together the egg yolks and sugar. Pour the cream into a saucepan and bring almost to a boil. Gradually stir the cream into the egg mixture. Strain the custard into the apples and mix well. Spoon into the pie shells, then bake for 15–20 minutes until the custard is set. Leave to cool.

4. About 25 minutes before serving, remove the pies from the pans. Overlap the apple slices on top, sprinkle with the remaining sugar and caramelize with a blowtorch.

Rose Petal
BRÛLÉE

POPULAR IN THE MIDDLE EAST, ROSE PETALS AND ROSEWATER HAVE BEEN USED TO FLAVOR BOTH SWEET AND SAVORY DISHES FOR CENTURIES.

8 egg yolks
¼ cup superfine sugar
2½ cups heavy cream
3 tablespoons rosewater

To finish
¼ cup superfine sugar
crystallized rose petals

1. Use a fork to mix together the egg yolks and sugar in a bowl. Pour the cream into a saucepan and slowly bring almost to a boil. Gradually mix it into the yolk mixture, stirring continuously.

2. Place 6 heatproof ramekins in a roasting pan. Strain the custard back into the saucepan, stir in the rosewater, then divide the flavored custard between the dishes. Pour warm water around the dishes to come halfway up the sides. Bake the custards in a preheated oven at 350°F for 20–25 minutes until they are just set with a slight softness at the center.

3. Leave the dishes to cool in the water, then lift them out and chill in the refrigerator for 3–4 hours. About 25 minutes before serving, sprinkle the tops of the desserts with the remaining sugar and caramelize with a blowtorch. Leave at room temperature until ready to serve. Serve decorated with crystallized rose petals.

Tips
As rosewater has a strong flavor, add it spoonful by spoonful and taste as you go.
You can make your own crystallized rose petals by brushing plain rose petals with a little reconstituted dried egg white and dusting with superfine sugar.

LAVENDER
BRÛLÉE

LAVENDER FLOWERS ADD A DELICATE FLAVOR TO THIS DESSERT AND CAPTURE THE ESSENCE OF SUMMER.

10–12 fresh or dried lavender flower stems, depending on size
2½ cups heavy cream
8 egg yolks
¼ cup superfine sugar
3 tablespoons confectioner's sugar, to finish
lavender flower stems, to decorate

Tips

As a variation, a few sprigs of fresh rosemary or a couple of bay leaves can be infused in the cream in the same way. Both taste delicious served with poached fresh or dried apricots or fresh orange segments.

1. Break the lavender flowers off their stems and put them in a saucepan. Pour the cream into the pan, then slowly bring almost to a boil. Remove from the heat and allow to stand for 15 minutes for the flavor to develop.

2. Use a fork to mix the egg yolks and sugar in a bowl. Reheat the cream, then gradually mix it into the yolks, stirring continuously.

3. Place 6 heatproof ramekins in a roasting pan and strain the custard into the dishes. Pour warm water around the dishes to come halfway up the sides and bake in a preheated oven at 350°F for 20–25 minutes, until the custards are set with a slight softness at the center.

4. Leave the dishes to cool in the water, then lift them out and transfer to the refrigerator for 3–4 hours to chill well. About 20–30 minutes before serving, sprinkle the custard tops with confectioner's sugar. Caramelize with a blowtorch, then leave at room temperature. Decorate with extra lavender stems to serve.

RASPBERRY AND CHAMPAGNE
BRÛLÉE

THIS BRÛLÉE HAS RUBY RED RASPBERRIES BATHED IN A SOFT BUBBLY ZABAGLIONE-STYLE CUSTARD—DEFINITELY A DESSERT TO IMPRESS.

2 cups (about 8 oz.) fresh raspberries
6 egg yolks
⅔ cup superfine sugar
½ cup dry Champagne
½ cup heavy cream
3 tablespoons confectioner's sugar, sifted, to finish
a few extra raspberries, dusted with confectioner's sugar, to decorate (optional)

1. Divide the raspberries between 6 ramekins or custard cups. Put the egg yolks and sugar in a large bowl and set it over a saucepan of simmering water, making sure that the water does not touch the bottom of the bowl. Whisk the egg yolks and sugar until light and foamy then gradually whisk in the Champagne and then the cream. Continue whisking for about 20 minutes until the custard is very thick and bubbly.

2. Pour the custard over the raspberries and leave to cool at room temperature for about 1 hour. Sprinkle the tops with sifted confectioner's sugar and caramelize with a blowtorch. Serve within 20–30 minutes, decorated with a few extra raspberries lightly dusted with confectioner's sugar, if liked.

Tip
Strawberries, or a mixture of raspberries and strawberries, are also delicious in this recipe, or diced mango and papaya for a dessert with a taste of the tropics.

Cranberry, ORANGE,
AND COINTREAU BRÛLÉE

SPECKLED WITH TANGY CRANBERRIES AND FLAVORED WITH THE ZEST OF AN ORANGE AND COINTREAU ORANGE LIQUEUR, THIS BRÛLÉE PACKS A PUNCH.

1½ cups (about 7 oz.) cranberries
1 orange, grated zest and juice
½ cup superfine sugar
8 egg yolks
2 cups heavy cream
2 tablespoons Cointreau
¼ cup superfine sugar, to finish

Tip
Grand Marnier, tequila, and even Galliano can be used instead of Cointreau, if you prefer.

1. Put the cranberries in a saucepan with the orange juice, reserving the zest for the custard, and cook over a medium heat for 5–8 minutes until the cranberries soften. Remove from the heat and stir in half the sugar.

2. Use a fork to mix together the egg yolks and the remaining sugar in a bowl. Pour the cream into a second saucepan and bring almost to a boil. Gradually stir it into the yolk mixture, then strain into the cooked cranberries, add the Cointreau, and mix together.

3. Arrange 6 ovenproof ramekins in a roasting pan. Pour in the cranberry custard, then pour warm water into the roasting pan to come halfway up the sides of the dishes. Bake in a preheated oven at 350°F for 25–30 minutes until the custards are set with a slight softness at the center.

4. Leave the dishes to cool in the water, then lift them out and chill in the refrigerator for 3–4 hours. About 20–30 minutes before serving, sprinkle the tops of the desserts with sugar and caramelize with a blowtorch. Leave at room temperature until ready to serve.

Marsala
BAKED PEACH
B R Û L É E

IF YOU HAVEN'T USED MARSALA BEFORE, IT'S WORTH SEEKING OUT. IT IS A FORTIFIED WINE WHICH COMPLEMENTS FRUIT AND CREAMY DESSERTS BEAUTIFULLY.

2 ripe peaches, halved and pitted
¼ cup Marsala
2 tablespoons superfine sugar
8 egg yolks
¼ cup superfine sugar
1½ cups heavy cream
1 cup mascarpone cheese
3 tablespoons superfine sugar, to finish

Tip
If you like, this custard can also be made with 2½ cups heavy cream instead of the heavy cream and mascarpone cheese mixture.

1. Thinly slice the peaches and put them in a saucepan with the Marsala and 2 tablespoons sugar. Cover and cook gently for 5 minutes until tender, then leave to cool.

2. Use a fork to mix together the egg yolks and remaining sugar in a bowl. Pour the cream into a saucepan, then bring almost to a boil. Gradually stir it into the egg mixture.

3. Put the mascarpone in a bowl, pour in the cooking liquid from the peaches, and beat together. Gradually strain in the warm custard and whisk until smooth.

4. Arrange 6 heatproof ramekins in a roasting pan. Pour the custard into the dishes, then pour warm water into the roasting pan to come halfway up the sides of the dishes. Bake in a preheated oven at 350°F for 20–25 minutes until set with a slight softness at the center. Leave the dishes to cool in the water, then chill in the refrigerator for 3–4 hours.

5. About 20–30 minutes before serving, arrange the peach slices over the tops of the desserts. Sprinkle with the remaining sugar and caramelize with a blowtorch. Leave at room temperature until ready to serve.

Amaretto Brûlée

FLAVORS DON'T HAVE TO BE COMPLICATED TO BE GOOD, AS THIS BRÛLÉE ILLUSTRATES. JUST A SIMPLE ADDITION OF A FEW TABLESPOONS OF THE ITALIAN LIQUEUR AMARETTO DI SARONNO AND A SCATTERING OF SLIVERED ALMONDS ON THE BRÛLÉE CREATE A WONDERFUL FLAVOR.

8 egg yolks
¼ cup superfine sugar
2½ cups heavy cream
½ cup Amaretto di Saronno

To finish
6 teaspoons slivered almonds
3 tablespoons confectioner's sugar

1. Use a fork to mix together the egg yolks and sugar in a bowl. Pour the cream into a saucepan and slowly bring almost to a boil, then gradually mix it into the yolk mixture.

2. Stir in the Amaretto, then strain the custard back into the saucepan.

3. Arrange 6 ramekins or custard cups in a roasting pan, then divide the custard between them. Pour warm water into the roasting pan to come halfway up the sides of the dishes and bake in a preheated oven 350°F for 20–25 minutes until the custards are just set with a slight softness at the center.

4. Leave the dishes to cool in the water, then chill in the refrigerator for 3–4 hours. About 20–30 minutes before serving, sprinkle the almonds over the desserts and sprinkle with the confectioner's sugar (no need to sift). Caramelize with a blowtorch, then leave at room temperature until you are ready to eat.

Sweet
EARL GREY
BRÛLÉE

THE ADDITION OF TEA MAKES DELICIOUS BRÛLÉES THAT WILL BE A GREAT TALKING POINT WITH DINNER GUESTS.

2½ cups light cream
8 teaspoons loose Earl Grey tea
8 egg yolks
½ cup superfine sugar
¼ cup superfine sugar, to finish

1. Pour the cream into a saucepan and bring almost to a boil. Remove from the heat, stir in the tea leaves, then allow to stand for 15 minutes for the tea to flavor the cream.

2. Beat the egg yolks and sugar in a bowl. Reheat the tea-flavored cream and gradually stir it into the egg mixture.

3. Arrange 6 ramekins or ovenproof teacups in a roasting pan and strain the custard into them. Pour warm water into the roasting pan to come halfway up the sides of the dishes and bake in a preheated oven at 350°F for 20–25 minutes until the custards are just set with a slight softness at the center.

4. Leave the dishes to cool in the water, then lift them out and chill in the refrigerator for 3–4 hours. About 20–30 minutes before serving, sprinkle the tops with the remaining sugar. Caramelize with a blowtorch, then leave at room temperature.

Honey and Pine Nut Brûlée

ALTHOUGH THE COMBINATION OF PINE NUTS AND HONEY IS MORE TRADITIONALLY SEEN IN FRANCE AS A TART FILLING, IT COMPLEMENTS A RICH CREAMY CUSTARD BRÛLÉE PERFECTLY.

8 egg yolks
3 tablespoons creamy honey
2½ cups heavy cream
1 lemon, grated zest only
⅓ cup pine nuts
3 tablespoons confectioner's sugar, to finish

Tip

For the best flavor, use creamy flower honey rather than clear.

1. Use a fork to mix together the egg yolks and honey in a bowl. Pour the cream into a saucepan and bring almost to a boil. Gradually beat it into the egg yolk mixture.

2. Strain the custard into a bowl, then stir in the lemon zest. Arrange 6 ramekins in a roasting pan, divide the pine nuts between the dishes, then top with the custard. Pour warm water into the roasting pan to come halfway up the sides of the dishes. Bake in a preheated oven at 350°F for 20–25 minutes or until the custard is set with a slight softness at the center.

3. Leave the dishes to cool in the water, then chill in the refrigerator for 3–4 hours. About 25 minutes before serving, sprinkle the tops of the desserts with confectioner's sugar (no need to sift) and caramelize with a blowtorch. Leave at room temperature until you are ready to serve.

Brûléed FIGS AND HONEY

FRESH FIGS HAVE SUCH A SHORT SEASON THAT IT IS WORTH ENJOYING THEM WHILE THEY ARE IN THE MARKETS OR, IF YOU ARE LUCKY ENOUGH, IN THE GARDEN.

9 fresh figs
4 tablespoons flower honey
8 egg yolks
2½ cups heavy cream
¼ cup superfine sugar, to finish

Tip
If you can't get fresh figs, use fresh apricots or 3 thickly sliced peaches instead.

1. Wash or peel the figs depending on the quality and thickness of the skins. Cut them into quarters and arrange cut side up in 6 shallow, 1¼-cup round heatproof dishes.

2. Beat together the honey and egg yolks in a bowl with a fork. Pour the cream into a saucepan and bring almost to a boil. Gradually beat the cream into the egg yolk mixture.

3. Arrange the dishes of figs in two roasting pans, then strain the custard into the dishes. Carefully pour warm water into the roasting pans to come halfway up the sides of the dishes. Bake the custards in a preheated oven at 350°F for 20–25 minutes until they are just set with a slight softness at the center.

4. Leave the dishes to cool in the water, then lift them out and chill in the refrigerator for 3–4 hours. About 20–30 minutes before serving, sprinkle the tops with the sugar. Caramelize with a blowtorch, then leave at room temperature.

No-Bake
LEMON
BRÛLÉE

2½ cups heavy cream
⅔ cup superfine sugar
2 lemons, grated zest of 1 and the juice of both
3 tablespoons confectioner's sugar, to finish
cookies or orange segments, to serve

Tip

Heavy cream will not curdle even if it is boiled, providing that it is stirred and cooked for no more than 2–3 minutes. Light cream on the other hand can only be brought to just below boiling point or it will start to curdle.

FRESH AND TANGY, THIS BRÛLÉE IS SIMPLICITY ITSELF TO MAKE. THE ADDITION OF THE LEMON JUICE THICKENS THE CREAM ALMOST AS IF BY MAGIC, SO THAT EGG YOLKS ARE NOT NECESSARY IN THIS RECIPE.

1. Pour the cream into a saucepan, add the sugar, and heat gently, stirring continuously, until the sugar has completely dissolved. Bring to a boil and cook for 2–3 minutes, stirring frequently.

2. Take the saucepan off the heat and stir in the lemon zest, then gradually mix in the juice. Pour the lemon cream into 6 ramekins or custard cups and leave to cool, then chill in the refrigerator for 3–4 hours until set.

3. About 25 minutes before serving, sprinkle the tops of the desserts with the confectioner's sugar. Caramelize with a blowtorch then leave at room temperature. Serve on small saucers with crisp cookies or orange segments.

Lime and
PAPAYA
BRÛLÉE

CRACK THE CRISP SUGARY SHELL OF THIS BRÛLÉE TO REVEAL A TANGY, SOFTLY SET LIME-SPECKLED CUSTARD WITH REFRESHING DICED PAPAYA UNDERNEATH.

1 papaya
8 egg yolks
¼ cup superfine sugar
2½ cups heavy cream
2 limes, grated zest of both, juice of 1
¼ cup superfine sugar, to finish

Tip
For a variation, use diced mango or fresh peaches instead of papaya.

1. Cut the papaya in half and scoop out the black seeds with a teaspoon. Remove the skin, then dice the flesh. Divide the flesh between 6 ramekins and place them in a roasting pan.

2. Use a fork to mix together the egg yolks and sugar in a bowl. Pour the cream into a saucepan, bring slowly almost to a boil, then gradually beat it into the egg yolk mixture.

3. Strain the custard back into the saucepan, stir in the lime zest and juice, then divide it between the dishes. Pour warm water into the roasting pan to come halfway up the side of the dishes. Bake the custards in a preheated oven at 350°F for 20–25 minutes until they are just set with a slight softness at the center.

4. Leave the dishes to cool in the water, then lift them out and chill in the refrigerator for 3–4 hours. About 25 minutes before serving, sprinkle the tops of the desserts with the sugar and caramelize with a blowtorch. Leave at room temperature until serving.

Warm
BERRY BRÛLÉE

BRÛLÉES DON'T ALWAYS NEED TO BE SERVED CHILLED. THIS COMFORTING MIXED RED BERRY DESSERT, FOR EXAMPLE, IS PARTICULARLY GOOD SERVED WARM. ALLOW THE RICH CUSTARD TO SETTLE AND COOL FOR ABOUT 1 HOUR, THEN CARAMELIZE THE TOPS AND SERVE. THE CONSISTENCY IS MUCH SOFTER THAN A CHILLED BRÛLÉE BUT THE FLAVOR IS JUST AS DELICIOUS.

1½ cups mixed red berries
8 egg yolks
⅓ cup superfine sugar
1 teaspoon vanilla extract
1 cup crème fraîche
1 cup heavy cream
¼ cup superfine sugar, to finish
selection of fresh berries dusted with confectioner's sugar, to serve

1. Arrange 6 ovenproof ramekins or custard cups in a roasting pan, then divide the berries between them. Use a fork to mix together the egg yolks, sugar, vanilla extract, and crème fraîche in a bowl. Pour the cream into a saucepan and bring almost to a boil. Gradually stir it into the yolk mixture.

2. Strain the mixture into the ramekins. Mix the fruits in the cream with a fork. Pour warm water into the roasting pan to come halfway up the side of the dishes, then bake in a preheated oven at 350°F for 25–30 minutes until the custards are set with a slight softness at the center.

3. Lift the dishes out of the water and leave at room temperature to cool for about 1 hour. Sprinkle the tops with the sugar and caramelize with a blowtorch. Serve within 30 minutes.

Tip
You could use all heavy cream for this recipe instead of the mixture of crème fraîche and heavy cream. In this case, warm all the cream in a saucepan before mixing it into the egg yolks.

SAFFRON
BRÛLÉE

SAFFRON ADDS A VIBRANT BURST OF GOLDEN COLOR AND AN EXOTIC, SWEET PUNGENCY TO THIS DELICIOUS DESSERT.

1½ cups heavy cream
1 cup light cream
½ teaspoon saffron threads
8 egg yolks
¼ cup superfine sugar
¼ cup superfine sugar, to finish

Tip
This brûlée is delicious served with a few blackberries dusted with a little sifted confectioner's sugar.

1. Pour the heavy and light creams into a saucepan, add the saffron threads, and slowly bring almost to a boil. Take off the heat and allow to stand for 15 minutes for the flavor to develop.

2. Use a fork to mix together the egg yolks and sugar in a bowl. Reheat the cream, then gradually mix it into the yolks, stirring continuously.

3. Place 6 heatproof ramekins or custard cups in a roasting pan, then strain the custard into them. Pour warm water into the roasting pan to come halfway up the sides of the dishes. Bake in a preheated oven at 350°F for 20–25 minutes, until the custards are just set with a slight softness at the center.

4. Leave the dishes to cool in the water, then lift them out and transfer to the refrigerator for 3–4 hours to chill well. About 20–30 minutes before serving, sprinkle the tops with the remaining sugar. Caramelize with a blowtorch, then leave at room temperature until ready to serve.

Iced BRÛLÉE

CREAMY SMOOTH ICE CREAM PEPPERED WITH TINY FLECKS OF REAL VANILLA, TOPPED WITH A BRITTLE, GLASSLIKE CARAMEL—HEAVEN ON A PLATE.

1 vanilla bean
1¼ cups whole milk
oil, for brushing
6 egg yolks
⅓ cup superfine sugar
1¼ cups heavy cream

Caramel
1 cup granulated sugar
1 cup water

1. Slit the vanilla bean lengthwise and put it in a saucepan. Pour in the milk, bring it almost to a boil, remove from the heat and allow to stand for 15 minutes.

2. Line a baking sheet with foil and with a pencil draw 6 circles using an upturned ramekin dish as a guide. Brush the foil with oil. Follow step 2 on page 44 to make the caramel, and pour a little into the center of each circle, so that it spreads to the outer edge.

3. Holding the vanilla bean against the side of the saucepan, scrape the black seeds into the milk. Discard the casing. Use a fork to mix the egg yolks and sugar together in a bowl, reheat the milk, then stir it into the yolk mixture. Return the custard to the pan and heat gently, stirring, until it coats the back of a spoon. Leave to cool.

4. Whip the cream until it forms soft peaks, then fold it into the custard. Pour into a shallow, nonstick loaf pan and freeze for 2 hours. Beat the ice cream with a fork, return it to the freezer for a further 2 hours, then beat again.

5. Line 6 ramekins with plastic wrap and spoon in the ice cream. Freeze for 2 hours or until solid.

6. Lift the ice creams out of the ramekins by pulling on the plastic wrap. Peel off the plastic. Set the ice creams on plates, peel off the sugar discs from the foil and place on the top of them.

BANOFFEE
BRÛLÉE

THIS LOOKS LIKE A STANDARD BRÛLÉE, BUT CRACK THROUGH THE CARAMELIZED SUGAR FOR A DELICIOUS SURPRISE.

oil, for brushing
4 egg yolks
¼ cup superfine sugar
1¼ cups whole milk
2 oz soft caramels
2 small bananas, sliced and tossed in 2 tablespoons lemon juice
3 teaspoons instant coffee granules or powder
1¼ cups heavy cream
a few tablespoons boiling water

Caramel
½ cup granulated sugar
½ cup water

1. Line a baking sheet with foil and with a pencil draw 6 circles using an upturned ramekin dish as a guide. Brush the foil with oil. Follow step 2 on page 44 to make the caramel, and pour a little into the center of each circle on the foil, so that it spreads to the outer edge of each one to form a disc.

2. Use a fork to mix the egg yolks with half the sugar. Pour the milk into a saucepan and bring almost to a boil. Gradually stir it into the yolk mixture, then strain back into the saucepan. Put the pan back on the heat, add the caramels and stir until they melt.

3. Arrange 6 heatproof ramekins in a roasting pan. Pour the custard into the dishes, then pour warm water into the roasting pan to come halfway up the sides of the dishes. Bake in a preheated oven at 350°F for 15–18 minutes until the custards are just set with a slight softness at the center.

4. Leave the dishes to cool in the water, then lift them out and chill in the refrigerator for 3 hours. Arrange the banana slices over the custard. Dissolve the coffee in the boiling water, then set aside.

5. Whip the cream until soft peaks form, then fold in the coffee and the remaining sugar. Divide the cream mixture between the dishes and even the tops with a knife or spatula. Chill for 1–2 hours. Peel the caramel discs off the foil and arrange on the desserts. Serve immediately.

Banana and Maple
BRÛLÉE

IF YOU WANT TO MAKE A BRÛLÉE BUT DON'T HAVE THE TIME TO BAKE AND CHILL ONE, THEN CHEAT AND MAKE THIS CREAMY SMOOTH VERSION WITH WHIPPED CREAM MIXED WITH THICK GREEK YOGURT AND FLAVORED WITH MASHED BANANAS AND MAPLE SYRUP.

1 cup heavy cream
½ cup thick, Greek-style yogurt
2 bananas
1 tablespoon lemon juice
4 tablespoons maple syrup
3 tablespoons soft light brown sugar, to finish

1. Whip the cream in a large bowl until it forms soft peaks, then fold in the yogurt. Peel and mash the bananas on a plate with a fork, then work in the lemon juice. Fold the bananas and maple syrup into the cream mixture.

2. Place 6 ramekins or custard cups on a small tray and divide the banana cream mixture between them. Smooth the surface of each one, then chill until ready to eat.

3. Just before serving, sprinkle the brown sugar over the tops of the desserts and caramelize with a blowtorch. Leave for a minute or two to harden, then serve.

Tip
Fresh lime juice may also be used to stop the banana discoloring, or bottled lemon juice, if you prefer.

Passion Fruit Brûlée

PASSION FRUIT SEEDS HAVE A UNIQUE AND DELICATE FLAVOR THAT MARRIES WELL WITH THE VELVETY SMOOTHNESS OF CUSTARD.

8 egg yolks
¼ cup superfine sugar
2½ cups heavy cream
6 passion fruit
1 lime, finely grated zest only
¼ cup superfine sugar, to finish

1. Use a fork to mix the egg yolks and sugar in a bowl. Pour the cream into a saucepan and bring almost to a boil, then gradually stir it into the yolk mixture.

2. Strain the custard into the saucepan. Halve the passion fruit and scoop the seeds into the custard with a teaspoon. Add the lime zest and mix together. Arrange 6 heatproof ramekins in a roasting pan, pour the custard into the dishes, then pour warm water into the roasting pan to come halfway up the sides of the dishes. Bake in a preheated oven at 350°F for 20–25 minutes until the custards are set with a slight softness at the center.

3. Leave the dishes to cool in the water, then lift them out and chill in the refrigerator for 3–4 hours. About 25 minutes before serving, sprinkle the tops of the desserts with the remaining sugar and caramelize with a blowtorch. Leave at room temperature until ready to serve.

COCONUT
AND GINGER
BRÛLÉE

8 egg yolks
¼ cup superfine sugar
1¼ fl. oz. canned coconut milk
¾ cup heavy cream
2 oz. crystallized ginger, drained and very
finely chopped
¼ cup superfine sugar, to finish

Tip

As a variation, substitute the grated zest of 2 limes
for the ginger.

FLAVORED WITH FINELY CHOPPED GINGER AND BATHED IN A SUBTLE AND SURPRISINGLY LIGHT COCONUT CUSTARD, THIS UNUSUAL BRÛLÉE IS AN IDEAL DESSERT AFTER A SPICY MAIN COURSE.

1. Use a fork to mix together the egg yolks and sugar in a bowl. Stir the coconut milk well, then pour it into a saucepan, add the cream, and bring almost to a boil. Gradually mix it into the egg yolks, then strain into the saucepan.

2. Stir the ginger into the coconut mixture. Arrange 6 ovenproof ramekins or custard cups in a roasting pan and fill with the coconut mixture. Pour warm water into the roasting pan to come halfway up the sides of the dishes, then bake in a preheated oven at 350°F for 20–25 minutes until the custards have set with a slight softness at the center.

3. Leave the dishes to cool in the water, then lift them out and chill for 3–4 hours. About 25 minutes before serving, sprinkle sugar over the top of each dessert and caramelize with a blowtorch until golden. Leave at room temperature until ready to eat.

CLOTTED CREAM
AND APRICOT BRÛLÉE

RICH CLOTTED CREAM MAKES THIS FRUITY BRÛLÉE EXTRA CREAMY. IT IS MADE ON THE STOVE RATHER THAN IN THE OVEN, TO GIVE A SOFTER, SPOONABLE TEXTURE.

1 cup ready-to-eat dried apricots
⅔ cup water
8 egg yolks
¼ cup superfine sugar
2 teaspoons cornstarch
1½ cups whole milk
2 tablespoons lemon juice
⅔ cup clotted cream
¼ cup superfine sugar, to finish

1. Put the apricots in a small saucepan with the water, cover, and cook gently for 10 minutes.

2. Meanwhile, use a fork to mix together the egg yolks, sugar, and cornstarch in a bowl. Pour the milk into a second saucepan and bring to a boil. Gradually beat it into the egg yolk mixture. Strain the mixture into the saucepan and bring back to a boil, reduce the heat, and cook very gently for 3–4 minutes, stirring continuously, until the custard thickly coats the back of the spoon.

3. Put the apricots in a food processor with half the custard and purée until smooth. Mix with the remaining custard and the lemon juice, then leave to cool.

4. Stir the clotted cream into the apricot mixture, then spoon into 6 ramekins set on a tray. Chill for 3–4 hours in the refrigerator until set. About 25 minutes before serving, sprinkle the tops of the desserts with the sugar and caramelize with a blowtorch. Leave at room temperature to harden and serve when ready.

RHUBARB
AND CUSTARD
BRÛLÉE

THIS COMFORTING DESSERT IS LIGHTER THAN A TRADITIONAL BRÛLÉE BECAUSE IT IS MADE WITH MILK INSTEAD OF CREAM. CHOOSE EARLY HOTHOUSE RHUBARB SO THAT THE FINISHED DESSERT IS FULL OF PRETTY PASTEL PINK LAYERS.

1 lb. fresh rhubarb, trimmed
½ cup superfine sugar
3 tablespoons water
8 egg yolks
3 teaspoons cornstarch
½ teaspoon vanilla extract
2 cups whole milk
3 tablespoons confectioner's sugar, to finish

1. Thinly slice the rhubarb and put it into a saucepan with half the sugar and the water and cook gently for 10 minutes until the rhubarb is tender but still bright pink. Cover and leave to cool.

2. Use a fork to mix together the egg yolks, the remaining sugar, cornstarch, and vanilla extract in a bowl. Pour the milk into a second saucepan and bring almost to a boil. Gradually stir the milk into the yolk mixture, then strain back into the saucepan. Bring the milk back to a boil, then reduce the heat and cook very gently for 3–4 minutes, stirring continuously, until the custard thickly coats the back of the spoon. Pour the custard into a bowl, cover with a saucer and leave to cool.

3. Arrange 6 ramekins or custard cups on a tray and fill with alternating spoonfuls of rhubarb and custard. Chill in the refrigerator for 3–4 hours.

4. About 25 minutes before serving, sprinkle the tops of the custards with the confectioner's sugar (no need to sift) and caramelize with a blowtorch. Leave at room temperature until serving.

Sweet PUMPKIN BRÛLÉE

THIS BRÛLÉE, WHICH IS DELICATELY SWEETENED WITH MAPLE SYRUP, IS RATHER LIKE A RICH PUMPKIN PIE FILLING WITHOUT THE CRUST. FRESH OR CANNED PURÉE CAN BE USED, OR BUTTERNUT SQUASH WHEN PUMPKIN IS OUT OF SEASON.

8 egg yolks
⅓ cup maple syrup
2 tablespoons light brown sugar
1 cup buttermilk
1 cup heavy cream
⅔ cup pumpkin purée
3 tablespoons light brown sugar, to finish

Tip

To make ⅔ cup pumpkin purée, steam 7 oz. pumpkin (weight after the peel and seeds have been removed) for 10 minutes, then purée in a food processor or blender until smooth.

1. Use a fork to mix together the egg yolks, maple syrup, and sugar in a bowl. Pour the buttermilk and cream into a saucepan and bring almost to a boil. Gradually mix the hot buttermilk mixture into the egg yolk mixture. Strain the custard back into the saucepan and stir in the pumpkin purée.

2. Place 6 individual heatproof ramekins in a roasting pan. Pour the custard mixture into the dishes, then pour warm water into the pan to come halfway up the sides of the dishes. Bake in a preheated oven at 350°F for 25–30 minutes until the desserts are just set with a slight softness at the center.

3. Leave the dishes to cool in the water, then lift them out and chill them in the refrigerator for 3–4 hours. About 25 minutes before serving, sprinkle the tops with the remaining sugar and caramelize with a blowtorch. Leave at room temperature until ready to eat.

Caramel
BRÛLÉE

RATHER THAN MIX THE CARAMEL SAUCE INTO THE BRÛLÉE CUSTARD, HERE IT HAS BEEN USED TO COAT THE RAMEKIN DISHES AND TOP THE DESSERTS.

oil, for brushing
1 cup granulated sugar
1 cup water
8 egg yolks
¼ cup superfine sugar
1 teaspoon vanilla extract
2½ cups heavy cream

1. Put 6 ovenproof ramekins in a preheated oven at 350°F.

2. Line a baking sheet with foil and with a pencil draw 6 circles using an upturned ramekin dish as a guide. Brush the foil with oil. To make the caramel, place the granulated sugar and water in a saucepan and slowly bring to a boil. Simmer gently, occasionally swirling the liquid in the pan, until it turns golden brown. Do not stir the caramel with a spoon.

3. Pour half the caramel into the warmed ramekins. Tilt the dishes to spread the caramel evenly over the bases and sides then put them into a roasting pan. With the remaining caramel, pour a little into the center of each circle on the foil, so that it spreads to the outer edge.

4. Use a fork to mix together the egg yolks, superfine sugar, and vanilla extract in a bowl. Pour the cream into a saucepan and bring almost to a boil, then gradually stir the cream into the yolk mixture. Strain the custard into the ramekins, then pour warm water into the roasting pan to come halfway up the sides of the dishes. Bake for 20–25 minutes until the desserts are set with a slight softness at the center.

5. Leave the dishes to cool in the water, then lift them out and chill in the refrigerator for 3–4 hours. To serve, ease the caramel discs off the baking sheet with a round-bladed knife and arrange on top of the desserts.

FUDGE
BRÛLÉE

THIS DESSERT IS PURE, SWEET INDULGENCE, SO ENJOY EVERY MOUTHFUL.

8 egg yolks
¼ cup light brown sugar, to finish

Fudge
1 cup granulated sugar
2 tablespoons water
½ cup (1 stick) unsalted butter, diced
2 cups heavy cream

1. To make the fudge, put the granulated sugar and water in a skillet and cook over a moderate heat until the sugar dissolves completely. Do not stir the sugar but instead tilt the skillet to mix any dry sugar with the syrup. Continue heating the syrup until it begins to turn golden, keeping a very close eye on it and tilting the skillet until all the syrup is evenly colored. This will take about 10 minutes.

2. Take the skillet off the heat and gradually stir in the diced butter. When the bubbles have completely subsided, gradually mix the cream in until smooth. If the fudge is not blending easily with the cream, return the pan to a very low heat and stir until completely mixed.

3. Leave the fudge to cool for 10 minutes, then gradually beat in the egg yolks one by one until completely mixed in. Arrange 6 ovenproof ramekins in a roasting pan. Strain the fudge mixture into a bowl, then pour into the dishes. Pour warm water into the roasting pan to come halfway up the sides of the dishes. Bake in a preheated oven at 350°F for 20–25 minutes until the custards are set with a slight softness at the center.

4. Leave the dishes to cool in the water, then chill in the refrigerator for 3–4 hours. About 20–30 minutes before serving, sprinkle the tops of the desserts with the sugar and caramelize with a blowtorch. Leave at room temperature until ready to serve.

Coffee
LIQUEUR
BRÛLÉE

THIS IS THE IDEAL DESSERT FOR THOSE DINNER GUESTS WHO USUALLY REFUSE DESSERT. PACKED WITH ALL THE STRENGTH OF GOOD COFFEE, IT MAKES THE PERFECT FINALE TO A MEAL.

8 egg yolks
1/3 cup superfine sugar
2½ cups heavy cream
6 teaspoons instant coffee granules or powder
3 tablespoons Kahlua, brandy, or whisky
3 tablespoons demerara or raw sugar, to finish

1. Use a fork to mix together the egg yolks and superfine sugar in a bowl. Pour the cream into a saucepan and bring almost to a boil. Gradually stir it into the egg yolk mixture.

2. Strain the custard back into the saucepan and stir in the coffee and liqueur and keep stirring until the coffee has dissolved completely.

3. Arrange 6 ovenproof ramekins in a roasting pan. Pour the custard into the dishes, then pour warm water into the roasting pan to come halfway up the sides of the dishes. Bake in a preheated oven at 350°F for 20–25 minutes until the custard is set with a slight softness at the center.

4. Leave the dishes to cool in the water, then chill in the refrigerator for 3–4 hours. About 25 minutes before serving, sprinkle the tops of the desserts with the demerara sugar and caramelize with a blowtorch. Leave at room temperature until you are ready to serve.

Tip
Be sure to use level measuring spoons when spooning out the coffee or the brûlées will taste too strong.

47

White Chocolate
MINT
BRÛLÉE

THIS WHITE CHOCOLATE BRÛLÉE HAS AN INTENSE PEPPERMINTY FLAVOR.

2½ cups heavy cream
7 oz. white chocolate, broken into pieces
6 egg yolks
¼ cup superfine sugar
2 oz. strong, hard white peppermints
3 tablespoons confectioner's sugar, to finish

Tip

Since white chocolate is milder in flavor, more is required than when using bittersweet chocolate as in the Chocolate Rum Truffle Brûlée. Peppermint extract can be used in place of the strong peppermints if you prefer. Add it half a teaspoon at a time and taste as you go.

1. Pour the cream into a saucepan and bring just to a boil. Remove from the heat and add the chocolate. Allow to stand for 5 minutes until melted, stirring from time to time, until well mixed.

2. Use a fork to mix together the egg yolks and sugar in a bowl. Gradually mix in the chocolate cream, then strain it back into the saucepan. Put the peppermints in a plastic bag and crush with a rolling pin. Stir them into the custard mixture.

3. Arrange 6 heatproof ramekins or custard cups in a roasting pan, then pour the chocolate custard into the dishes. Pour warm water into the roasting pan to come halfway up the sides of the dishes. Bake in a preheated oven at 350°F for 20–25 minutes until custard is set with a slight softness at the center.

4. Leave the dishes to cool in the water, then lift out and chill in the refrigerator for 3–4 hours. About 20–30 minutes before serving, sprinkle the confectioner's sugar over the top of the desserts. Caramelize with a blowtorch and leave at room temperature until ready to serve.

Chocolate
RUM TRUFFLE
BRÛLÉE

THIS IS THE BRÛLÉE FOR ALL CHOCOLATE
LOVERS—DECADENT AND DELICIOUS.

2½ cups heavy cream
4 oz. bittersweet chocolate, broken into pieces
6 egg yolks
⅓ cup superfine sugar
3 tablespoons rum

To finish
2 oz. bittersweet chocolate
2 oz. white chocolate
½ cup heavy cream

1. Pour the cream into a saucepan and bring to a boil. Take the pan off the heat, add the bittersweet chocolate, and allow to stand for 5 minutes until the chocolate has melted, stirring occasionally.

2. Use a fork to mix together the egg yolks, sugar, and rum in a bowl. Reheat the chocolate cream, then slowly beat it into the yolk mixture.

3. Arrange 6 ramekins in a roasting pan. Strain the chocolate mixture back into the saucepan, then pour it into the dishes. Pour warm water into the roasting pan to come halfway up the sides of the dishes and bake in a preheated oven at 350°F for 20–25 minutes until the custards are just set with a slight softness at the center.

4. Leave the dishes to cool in the water, then chill in the refrigerator for 3–4 hours.

5. To make the decoration, break the bittersweet chocolate into a bowl and set it over a saucepan of water that has just boiled and allow to melt. Line a baking sheet with parchment paper. Stir the melted chocolate, then spoon it into a parchment paper or plastic piping bag. Roll down the top and snip off the tip, then pipe squiggly, random lines on the parchment paper. Melt the white chocolate in the same way, then pipe squiggly lines over the bittersweet chocolate and between the gaps for a lacy effect. Chill until hard. To serve, whip the cream until it forms soft peaks, then spoon it over the desserts. Break the chocolate decoration into pieces and stick them into the cream.

CHOCOLATE MERINGUE BRÛLÉE

THIS IS A DESSERT THAT THE WHOLE FAMILY CAN ENJOY.

6 egg yolks
¼ cup superfine sugar
1½ cups heavy cream
1 cup whole milk
4 oz. bittersweet chocolate

Topping
3 egg whites
⅓ cup superfine sugar
a few mini marshmallows, to decorate

1. Use a fork to mix together the egg yolks and sugar in a bowl. Pour the cream and milk into a saucepan and bring almost to a boil. Gradually beat it into the yolk mixture. Strain the mixture back into the saucepan.

2. Break the chocolate into pieces, and stir them into the custard. Set aside for 5 minutes, stirring occasionally, until the chocolate has completely melted.

3. Arrange 6 ovenproof ramekins in a roasting pan, then strain the custard into them. Pour warm water into the roasting pan to come halfway up the sides of the dishes and bake in a preheated oven at 350°F for 15 minutes.

4. Meanwhile, whisk the egg whites in a bowl until they form stiff, moist-looking peaks. Gradually whisk in the sugar, a spoonful at a time, and continue whisking until the egg whites are smooth and glossy. Carefully take the roasting pan out of the oven, spoon the meringue on top of the custards and swirl with the back of the spoon. Return the custards to the oven for 8–10 minutes until the topping is golden brown and set.

5. Leave the dishes to cool in the water, then lift them out and chill in the refrigerator for 3–4 hours. Decorate with mini marshmallows just before serving.

TRIPLE
CHOCOLATE
BRÛLÉE

THIS NO-BAKE BRÛLÉE IS SERIOUSLY RICH AND MADE WITH THREE CONTRASTING LAYERS OF CHOCOLATE.

8 egg yolks
¼ cup superfine sugar
2½ cups heavy cream
4 oz. bittersweet chocolate, finely chopped
4 oz. white chocolate, finely chopped
4 oz. milk chocolate, finely chopped
3 tablespoons Amaretto di Saronno or brandy (optional)
¼ cup superfine sugar, to finish
bittersweet, white, and milk chocolate curls, to decorate (optional)

1. Use a fork to mix together the egg yolks and sugar in a bowl. Pour the cream into a saucepan and bring almost to a boil. Gradually beat the cream into the yolk mixture.

2. Strain the custard into a liquid measuring cup, then divide it equally between 3 bowls. Stir a different chocolate into each bowl of hot custard, adding a tablespoon of liqueur, if using. Stir until melted.

3. Divide the bittersweet chocolate custard between 6 ramekins. When cool, transfer the dishes to the freezer for 10 minutes to chill and set.

4. Take the dishes out of the freezer, stir the white chocolate custard, and spoon it over the dark layer in the dishes. Return to the freezer for 10 minutes.

5. Take the dishes out of the freezer, stir the milk chocolate custard, and spoon it into the dishes. Chill the custards in the refrigerator for 3–4 hours until set. About 25 minutes before serving, sprinkle the tops of the dishes with the remaining sugar and caramelize with a blowtorch. Leave at room temperature until ready to eat, then decorate with chocolate curls if desired.

Salmon
AND
SCALLION
BRÛLÉE

DELICATELY FLAVORED WITH SCALLIONS, PARSLEY, AND LEMON JUICE, THIS BRÛLÉE IS GENEROUSLY FLECKED WITH MOIST PIECES OF STEAMED SALMON.

10 oz. salmon fillet
4 scallions, thinly sliced
8 egg yolks
1 cup heavy cream
1 cup whole milk
3 tablespoons chopped parsley
2 tablespoons lemon juice
salt and pepper
¼ cup finely grated Parmesan cheese, to finish

Tip
Gruyère, Cheddar, or fontina cheese can be substituted for fresh Parmesan.

1. Rinse the salmon in cold water, then cook in a covered steamer for 8–10 minutes until the fish is the same color throughout and flakes easily when pressed with a knife. Meanwhile, steam the scallions for 1 minute or until softened.

2. Flake the salmon, discarding the skin and any bones. Divide the salmon and steamed scallions between 6 ovenproof ramekins or custard cups, then put the dishes into a roasting pan.

3. Use a fork to mix the egg yolks and salt and pepper in a bowl. Pour the cream and milk into a saucepan and bring almost to a boil, then gradually beat it into the yolk mixture and strain back into the saucepan. Stir in the parsley and lemon juice. Pour the custard over the salmon and mix gently with a fork. Pour warm water into the pan to come halfway up the sides of the dishes and bake in a preheated oven at 350°F for 20–25 minutes until the custards are set but with a slight softness at the center.

4. Leave the dishes to cool in the water, then lift them out and chill in the refrigerator for 3–4 hours. Just before serving, sprinkle the tops with the grated cheese. Melt and brown the cheese with a blowtorch, then serve immediately.

LOBSTER AND Tarragon BRÛLÉE

WONDERFULLY LUXURIOUS, THIS IS A BRÛLÉE FOR VERY SPECIAL OCCASIONS. AS IT IS SO RICH, SERVE THE BRÛLÉES ON LITTLE PLATES WITH A MIXED-LEAF SALAD.

1 large or 2 small freshly cooked lobsters
2 tablespoons chopped tarragon
8 egg yolks
2 tablespoons lemon juice
1 cup heavy cream
1 cup whole milk
salt and pepper

To finish
2 tablespoons fine white breadcrumbs
3 tablespoons finely grated mild Cheddar or fontina cheese

1. Twist off the claws and pincers from the lobster, then twist off the tail. Using scissors, cut down the length of the tail on the underside, discard the black, threadlike intestine from the center, then remove the white lobster meat. Gently crack open the claws with a mallet and take out the flesh. Cut the body of the lobster in half, remove the greenish-black sac from just behind the head, then pull away the meat from the body.

2. Divide the lobster between 6 ovenproof ramekins, sprinkle with the tarragon, then place the dishes in a roasting pan. Use a fork to mix together the egg yolks, lemon juice, and salt and pepper. Pour the cream and milk into a saucepan and bring almost to a boil. Gradually stir into the yolk mixture, then strain back into the saucepan.

3. Divide the custard between the dishes, then pour warm water into the roasting pan to come halfway up the sides of the dishes. Bake in a preheated oven at 350°F for 20–25 minutes until the custards are set with a slight softness at the center.

4. Leave the dishes to cool in the water, then lift them out and chill in the refrigerator for 3–4 hours. About 25 minutes before serving, sprinkle the tops of the custards with breadcrumbs and cheese and brown with a blowtorch. Leave at room temperature until you are ready to serve.

CARAMELIZED
ONION AND GRUYÈRE
BRÛLÉE

TRANSFORM THE HUMBLE ONION INTO A GOURMET EXTRAVAGANZA BY SAUTÉING IT, MIXING IT WITH THYME, GRATED SWISS CHEESE, AND A DELICIOUS CUSTARD.

2 tablespoons (¼ stick) butter
2 tablespoons olive oil
13 oz. onions, thinly sliced
2 teaspoons superfine or granulated sugar
6 egg yolks
1 teaspoon Dijon or mild mustard
2 tablespoons chopped thyme
1 cup heavy cream
1 cup whole milk
1 cup Gruyère cheese, finely grated
salt and pepper

To serve
melba toast
watercress or arugula garnish

1. Heat the butter and oil in a sauté pan, then gently sauté the onions for 10 minutes, stirring occasionally, until softened and just beginning to brown. Sprinkle the sugar over the onions, increase the heat slightly and sauté for 5 minutes, stirring frequently, until the onions are golden brown. Take off the heat and set aside.

2. Beat the egg yolks, mustard, thyme, and salt and pepper in a bowl. Pour the cream and milk into a saucepan and bring almost to a boil, then gradually beat into the egg yolk mixture. Set aside 4 tablespoons each of the grated cheese and the caramelized onions for the brûlée topping, then stir the rest into the yolk mixture.

3. Spoon the mixture into 6 ramekins set in a roasting pan. Pour warm water into the pan to come halfway up the sides of the dishes. Bake in a preheated oven at 350°F for 25–30 minutes until the custards are set with a slight softness at the center.

4. Leave the dishes to cool in the water for 2 hours. Just before serving, sprinkle the tops with the reserved cheese and onions and melt the cheese with a blowtorch. Serve with melba toast and a watercress or arugula garnish.

MINI SPINACH AND TOMATO LASAGNA
BRÛLÉE

5 oz. young spinach leaves, washed
3 tomatoes, skinned and finely chopped
1–2 garlic cloves, crushed
6 egg yolks
2 cups heavy cream
5 sheets dried lasagna, cooked in water until just tender
salt and pepper
¼ cup finely grated Parmesan cheese, to finish

1. Half fill the base of a steamer with water, bring it to a boil, and place the steamer top in position. Add the spinach, cover, and steam for 2–3 minutes. Mix the tomatoes with the garlic and salt and pepper.

2 . Use a fork to mix the egg yolks in a bowl with salt and pepper. Pour the cream into a

THIS IS A MUCH LIGHTER AND MORE COLORFUL ALTERNATIVE TO THE TRADITIONAL MEAT-FILLED LASAGNA.

saucepan and bring almost to a boil. Slowly stir into the egg yolks, then strain back into the saucepan.

3. Arrange 6 heatproof ramekins in a roasting pan. Cut the lasagna into strips the width of the dishes. Divide half the spinach between the dishes, cover with a spoonful of custard, then a layer of lasagna, curling the edges up the side of the dishes if necessary. Divide all the tomatoes between the dishes, then add a little custard and cover with a layer of lasagna. Add the rest of the spinach, a little custard, and a layer of lasagna. Pour on the rest of the custard.

4. Pour warm water into the roasting pan to come halfway up the sides of the dishes and bake them in a preheated oven at 350°F for 20–25 minutes until the custards are set. Leave the dishes to cool in the water for 1 hour. Lift the dishes out of the roasting pan, sprinkle the tops with Parmesan, and brown with a blowtorch.

Mushroom AND RICE BRÛLÉE

DRIED MUSHROOMS ADD AN INTENSITY OF FLAVOR TO THIS RISOTTO-BASED BRÛLÉE THAT CANNOT BE ACHIEVED BY FRESH MUSHROOMS ALONE.

1 cup (¾ oz.) dried mixed mushrooms
1 cup just boiled water
2 tablespoons olive oil
1 small onion, finely chopped
6 closed cup mushrooms, about 3½ oz.,
roughly chopped
2 garlic cloves, crushed
½ cup risotto rice
2 cups hot vegetable or chicken stock
4 egg yolks
1 cup heavy cream
salt and pepper
6 teaspoons superfine sugar, to finish

1. Put the dried mushrooms in a bowl, cover with the boiling water, and leave to soak for 15 minutes. Heat the oil in a saucepan and sauté the onion for 4–5 minutes until softened. Add the fresh mushrooms and garlic and cook for 2 minutes.

2. Lift the dried mushrooms out of the soaking water, reserving the water, and slice thinly. Add them to the saucepan with the rice and cook, stirring, for 1 minute. Add the soaking liquid, a little of the stock, and some salt and pepper. Simmer for 15 minutes, stirring occasionally, and adding more stock as necessary until the rice is tender.

3. Take the pan off the heat. Mix together the egg yolks and cream, then stir them into the risotto. Spoon into 6 ovenproof ramekins set in a roasting pan and pour in warm water to come halfway up the sides of the dishes. Bake in a preheated oven at 350°F for 15–20 minutes until piping hot.

4. Lift the dishes out of the roasting pan. Sprinkle the sugar over the tops of the brûlées, then caramelize with a blowtorch and serve immediately.

Tip
An alternative to a sweet topping is to sprinkle the brûlées with a little grated cheese instead. This brûlée is cooked for a slightly shorter time than the other recipes so that the rice does not dry out.

Roquefort
AND LEEK
BRÛLÉE

SOFT BLUE CHEESE COMBINED WITH THE MILD ONION FLAVOR OF LEEK FORMS THE BASE OF THIS DELICIOUS CUSTARD.

1 leek, about 8 oz., trimmed, halved lengthwise, well washed and thinly sliced
3½ oz. Roquefort cheese, cubed
8 egg yolks
2 cups light cream
1–2 garlic cloves, crushed (optional)
salt and pepper

To finish
3 tablespoons fine white breadcrumbs
2 tablespoons melted butter

1. Plunge the leeks into a saucepan of boiling water and cook for 2 minutes until softened. Drain, rinse with cold water, drain again, then pat dry with paper towels.

2. Divide half the leeks between 6 ovenproof ramekins and cover with half the cheese. Repeat with one more layer of each.

3. Use a fork to mix the eggs in a bowl with salt and pepper. Pour the cream into a saucepan and bring almost to a boil. Gradually stir the cream into the egg yolks. Strain the mixture back into the saucepan, then add the garlic, if using.

4. Place the dishes in a roasting pan, pour the custard into them, and mix lightly with a fork. Pour warm water into the roasting pan to come halfway up the sides of the dishes and bake them in a preheated oven at 350°F for 20–25 minutes until the custards are just set with a slight softness at the center.

5. Leave the dishes to cool in the water, then lift them out of the pan and chill in the refrigerator for 3–4 hours. About 30 minutes before serving, mix together the breadcrumbs and butter. Divide the topping between the dishes and brown with a blowtorch. Leave at room temperature until you are ready to serve.

Goat Cheese
AND
SUN-DRIED TOMATO
BRÛLÉE

DOTTED WITH JUST-MELTED PIECES OF GOAT CHEESE, SUN-DRIED TOMATOES, AND BLACK OLIVES, THIS BRÛLÉE CAPTURES THE FULL FLAVORS OF THE MEDITERRANEAN.

4 oz. goat cheese
10 pieces (5 oz.) sun-dried tomatoes in oil, drained
12 pitted black olives (optional)
8 egg yolks
1 cup whole milk
1 cup heavy cream
salt and pepper
¼ cup finely grated Parmesan cheese, to finish
warm ciabatta bread, to serve

Tip
Choose the sharper goat cheese sold in a log for maximum flavor.

1. Arrange 6 heatproof ramekins in a roasting pan. Cut the cheese into 6 slices, then crumble a slice into each dish. Thinly slice the tomatoes and roughly chop the olives, if using, then divide them between the dishes.

2. Use a fork to mix the egg yolks in a bowl with a little salt and pepper. Pour the milk and cream into a saucepan and bring almost to a boil. Gradually stir it into the egg yolks, then strain the mixture back into the saucepan.

3. Pour the custard into the dishes, then gently stir to mix in the cheese, tomatoes, and olives. Pour warm water into the roasting pan to come halfway up the sides of the dishes. Bake in a preheated oven at 350°F for 20–25 minutes until the custard is set with a slight softness at the center.

4. Leave the dishes to cool in the water, then lift them out and chill in the refrigerator for 3–4 hours. About 25 minutes before serving, sprinkle the tops with the cheese and brown with a blowtorch. Serve with the bread.

INDEX